Amazing Americans

Pocahontas

Sharon Coan, M.S.Ed.

There once was an
American Indian girl.

She was a princess.

Her name was
Pocahontas.

Her name means
playful.

One day a ship came
to America.

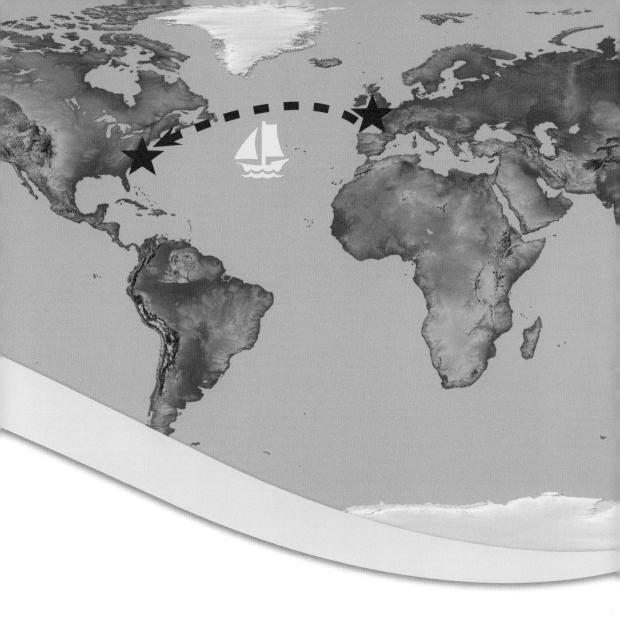

It was from England.

There were people
on the ship.

They were called **settlers**.

Pocahontas was nice
to them.

She helped them.

She married one of them.

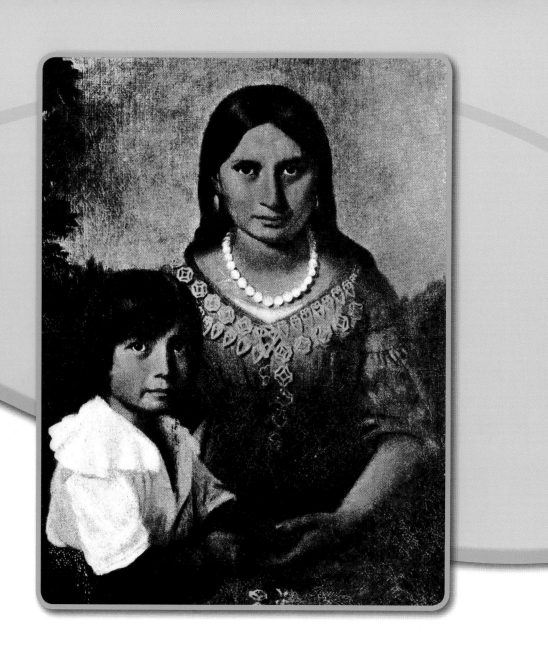

She had a son.

She went to England.

She met new people.

Pocahontas helped people get along.

She was a good
person.

Ask It!

Pocahontas was an amazing American. Ask an adult to help you find an amazing American.

Brandi and Alice

Alice thinks Brandi is an amazing American. Brandi is Alice's mom. She helps women all over the world. She shows them ways to make their lives better.

Ask how he or she helps people.

Glossary

American Indian— one of the first people to live in America

playful—happy and fun

settlers—people who go and live in a new place

Index

Your Turn!

Pretend you could talk to Pocahontas. What would you talk about? Draw your ideas.

Consultants

Shelley Scudder
Gifted Teacher
Broward County Schools

Caryn Williams, M.S.Ed.
Madison County Schools
Huntsville, AL

Publishing Credits

Conni Medina, M.A.Ed., *Managing Editor*
Lee Aucoin, *Creative Director*
Torrey Maloof, *Editor*
Lexa Hoang, *Designer*
Stephanie Reid, *Photo Editor*
Rachelle Cracchiolo, M.S.Ed., *Publisher*

Image Credits: Cover, pp.1, 23 (bottom) Glasshouse Images/Alamy; Backcover Ian Dagnall/Alamy; p.18 INTERFOTO/Alamy; pp.6, 13 North Wind Picture Archives/Alamy; p.24 The Protected Art Archive/Alamy; p.2 Chronicle/Alamy; p.23 (top) Thomas Sully/ Virginia Historical Society/The Bridgeman Art Library; pp.5, 10 Blue Lantern Studio/ Corbis; pp.8–9, 11–12, 14, 16 The Granger Collection, New York/The Granger Collection; p.17 chpaquette/iStockphoto; p.3 KIHN, W. LANGDON/National Geographic Stock; p.15 North Wind Picture Archives; All other images from Shutterstock.

Teacher Created Materials
5301 Oceanus Drive
Huntington Beach, CA 92649-1030
http://www.tcmpub.com
ISBN 978-1-4333-7353-4
© 2014 Teacher Created Materials, Inc.
Printed in China
Nordica.062018.CA21800491